Make Your Writing Bloom

A 7-Day Journey for Replanting Zest in Your Writing

Shonell Bacon

ChickLitGurrl
http://chicklitgurrl.com

ISBN-13: 978-1724813770
ISBN-10: 1724813773

Cover design by Samara King

Ordering Information:
Quantity sales. Special discounts are available on quantity purchases by corporations, associations, and others. For details, contact the publisher at the email address above.

Printed in the United States of America

Published by ChickLitGurrl, Lake Charles, LA

Visit www.chicklitgurrl.com

DEDICATION

To Brenda Henson, my mother and #1 supporter.

CONTENTS

ACKNOWLEDGMENTS

First, I thank my Lord and Savior, Jesus Christ, because without Him, I would not have the unwavering connection to God, who created me and gave me the gifts of writing and of teaching others about writing.

I give much love and thanks to my immediate family: my mother Brenda Henson; my brothers, Anthony and Michael; my sister Josette; my sister from another mister, author Samara King (thank you for my beautiful cover!); and my talented daughter Ceria LeDay. It's always so important to have people who love and support your passions, and I'm blessed to have this crew.

I *must* say thank you to the wonderful writer and all-around phenomenal woman, Bernice McFadden. She is my favorite author, and I was all set to be rejected when I asked her if she could read MYWB and write a blurb for it. I am so very honored that she said yes. I cannot say thank you enough!

There are so many people I could list here: my sisterfriends, my colleagues, my clients, and my students—all have played a role in me becoming the person who penned this work. Thank you all.

I WROTE THIS BOOK BECAUSE...

Think about your most exciting writing session. Imagine your hand clasped around a pen as you scribble furiously on the page or your fingertips burning a keyboard as the words seem to pour from you. Think about the wondrous blend of your characters' voices and the actions that take place as you write—and the fact that you actually like what you are writing. Think about how you feel during this moment. If you're like me, your heart is pounding, you're smiling hard, you're pumping a fist in the air, you *feel* like a writer. A good writer. A writer who has stories to tell and has the creative ability to do so.

Now, imagine the dip in the roller-coaster ride of writing. You know what I'm talking about.

The dark side of being a writer. On this side, writer's block dwells. If you're lucky, it doesn't last long. But its duration is the least of your problems because simply having it can be torturous.

Ever heard of the phrase "You never miss the water till the well runs dry"?

It's a perfect analogy for writer's block. When the ease of writing stops, we want nothing more than to dip our fingers in the writing well and spin stories again. However, we find our well bone dry. Creativity flatlined. You try to reread your story so that you can jump back into it. Doesn't work. You rifle through your huge writing folder to find a story idea that sparks you. Nothing generates a flicker. You even think about taking part in other creative endeavors with the hope of sparking your writing. It doesn't help at all. In desperation, you cry out, "One idea, thought? Something?"

Crickets are your response.

When you are a writer, when you are someone who feels as if you were born to write, writer's block can feel like death. It affects not only your creative output, but also your mind, your body, and your spirit. You begin to question whether you're supposed to be a writer. You question whether your writing, past and present, is any good. You start to look at other people who write and wonder why they can do it well and you can't. You start to question your creative ability, and sometimes even jealousy can creep in, especially when you're around a lot of prolific writers, and your writing seems to have packed up and left.

> **Writing (or not writing) affects your body, mind, and spirit.**

The sadness you feel, the jealousy you feel, the depression you feel, the anger and anxiety you feel for having not written—all these things affect your body. These emotions affect how you think, and they affect how you talk about yourself and the work you do. And if you have loved ones, these emotions affect them because there is nothing like living with a cranky writer, especially a cranky writer who can't write.

But here's the thing that should make you feel better: that block has an incoming rainstorm, a torrential downpour that will drench the dry creative lands and regrow a desire to write and write well.

Even though writer's block can be painful to endure, sometimes, the block is important because it's telling us that we need to pause from our writing so that we can refill: refill experiences, thoughts, emotions, and actions and take in the world so that we have more material that we can use to develop complex, intricate, and well-developed stories. Thinking about writer's block this way presents the opportunity for us to use that time in other creative ways, such as the collecting of experiences, so that our writing well is replenished.

> **Writer's block can be a symptom to a larger problem: an empty experience well.**

This book aims to be the help you need to reclaim your zest for writing.

Make Your Writing Bloom (MYWB) will give you tools to help you kick-start your writing and feel that excitement and adrenaline rush from having written great prose.

Because I love the number seven and the meaning of completeness that is associated with it, I designed MYWB as a seven-day journey to exploring your relationship with writing and reconnecting you to that relationship. Each chapter represents a day of your weeklong journey. You should set aside time every day during the week to reflect, meditate, and journal on the topics presented within the book.

What is your most comforting place to be when you think/write? What are the most comforting, creativity-inducing sounds to have around when you think/write? Do you have snacks? Drinks? Create a space that denotes PRO-YOU and PRO-WRITING.

For the next seven days, you will reflect and journal on the following seven topics:

> → Day 1: The Love of Writing
> → Day 2: Favorite Writing Experience
> → Day 3: Fears That Usurp Writing
> → Day 4: Daily Goings-on That Usurp Writing
> → Day 5: Blending Writing into a Busy Life
> → Day 6: Picking a Story Idea
> → Day 7: Road Trip to Writing

Journaling pages are in each chapter, and a Notes section is at the end of the book. There are also an extra few to-dos for the 30 days following our weeklong trip because this is not just about rediscovering your writing; it's also about *cultivating* a LIFETIME of good writing. So, let's get started.

DAY 1
THE LOVE OF WRITING

When I was 10 years old, my mother bought me a diary. She and I were spending a Saturday morning walking a flea market across the street from my grandparents' house. It's there I spotted the green faux leather diary. It had the word "Diary" in gold letters and came with a lock and key. My mom gave the man a quarter, and I left holding that diary.

Now, at age 10, it's not unusual for girls to start liking boys and having crushes. And with a diary, they would be quick to write cute things about these crushes.

This was *not* me.

I used that diary to write sports articles. Coming from Baltimore, I am a lifelong Baltimore Orioles fan, so I clipped pictures of Orioles players from the newspaper, taped them in my diary, and wrote stories about them. Even now, I smile at the memories because I wrote about something I loved, and in doing that, I remembered all the weekends that I spent sitting in front of the huge TV console with my granddad to cheer on the O's.

In addition to my "sports writing," I wrote scripts for the soap opera *The Guiding Light*. When I came home from school, before I started homework, the first thing I did was watch this soap opera. Long live Reva and Josh! Because I was so in love with the show, I began writing my own fan-fic scripts.

Before I was 10, I liked to write, but I loved to sing more. Getting that diary and being able to conjure up different stories about people excited me and grew my love for writing.

Throughout my teen years, that diary would transform into typewriters and then a Brother word processor that I bought with my first tax return money. On the machine, I wrote so many extraordinarily horrible screenplays all about baseball and romance. In almost every story, some female somehow became an integral cog of a baseball team and ended up falling in love with the star player. What can I say? I'm a girl who loves love and adores baseball.

That decade of writing, from my diary to my word processor, fostered in me this idea that writing should be and needs to be a significant part of my life. Even during the horrible times in which I started submitting work to agents and publishers and received enough rejection letters to wallpaper an entire home, there was still the burning desire in me to write.

Make Your Writing Bloom

Writing for me is cathartic. It is a vacation from the here and now. It allows me to be, at least through my characters, anything I can imagine. It enables me to tap into readers' emotions, desires, and needs, and to satisfy it all with the written word.

It is important for us to remember that desire, to remember why we love the art of writing. If we don't have that burn, that drive, that remembrance of how much it means to us to put words on the page, to create a story out of these words, it will be hard for us to write anything.

> **You may lose your writing relationship if you don't remember your love for writing.**

So, for Day 1, we are going to focus on LOVE. Your goal will be to think on and journal about the following question: **why do I love to write?**

This is not the time to think about the current situation, that is, the situation where you are not writing and you feel your desire is long gone. This is a time to think about your past writing experiences. Why did you start writing? How do you feel when the writing flows well? What do you think about yourself and your writing during these moments?

Take 10 to 15 minutes to think about these questions and any other thoughts and ideas that come about when you think about *your love of writing*.

Then, using the space below, take about 15 to 20 minutes to journal your responses.

If you're up for sharing, I would love to read your response! You can find me on Facebook and/or Twitter (contact info at end of book!) to share your response. When you share your journaling, be sure to add the following hashtags: #writingbloom and #loveofwriting.

____

____

____

____

____

____

____

____

____

____

____

____

Make Your Writing Bloom

Make Your Writing Bloom

DAY 2
FAVORITE WRITING EXPERIENCE

While pursuing my master's degree in mass communication, I took a novel writing course as an elective. It would be my first foray into understanding the innerworkings of fiction writing. It would also be the event that would create my favorite writing experience.

At the start of the course, my instructor asked each of us to do two things:

1. First, we needed to choose an idea for a novel we would begin writing during the course.
2. Then, using our idea's genre, we would select a published novel that had a lot of the style we wanted to create in our novel. So, for example, if your goal was to write a romance novel, then you might select a novel from your favorite romance author.

Once we completed these two activities, the real work began as the instructor explained the course's two major components.

Make Your Writing Bloom

Analyze Selected Novel

The first component I had to tackle involved reading my chosen novel and then writing analytical papers on various aspects of the story, such as plot, setting, character, dialogue, and scene development. The theory was that by analyzing the novel, I would learn more about the writing craft and hopefully apply what I learned to my own writing. With the weekly lectures and discussions on these elements of fiction, we all had the proper terminology to analyze our novels.

Write Beginning of Own Novel

For the second component of the class, I had to write the first three chapters of my novel with the thought being that as I was studying the writing craft and analyzing a book within the genre in which I would write, I would be set up well to dig in and write my story.

It really was kismet that this course came along when it did. At the time, I had a desire to write mysteries, but with that came the fear of writing them. You know— anything new can make you fearful of the *What ifs*. What if the writing sucks? What if everyone hates it— including your mother? Taking this course would force me to deal with those fears because if I didn't, I would fail the course. And I didn't like bad grades.

So, swallowing (and trying to keep down) my fears, I decided to write a mystery. I had a few loose pages of notes and figured, if not now, when?

Having selected mystery as my genre, it was an easy decision as to what book I would analyze: Mary Higgins Clark's *All Around the Town* (AATT). Clark is my most favorite mystery and suspense author, and AATT is a book I had read at least once a year since its release. I knew in analyzing it I would learn techniques and style that would help me in crafting my own story.

With weathered paperback in hand, I took to note taking, highlighting Clark's novel as I began to write my own: *Death at the Double Inkwell* (DDIW), the book that would end up being my first mystery written and published.

Write in a genre you've never written in before. You may discover another layer of your talent.

During the 15 weeks of the class, I managed to write the first three chapters of DDIW and to develop a solid outline for the rest of the novel. I received great reviews from my instructor and classmates, and was eager to continue with the novel upon the class' completion.

Even though there were moments when I doubted myself—in the class and after it—my experience of writing DDIW was phenomenal. My number one favorite genre to read is mystery, and I wanted the opportunity to write a mystery that would be intriguing to others. In writing DDIW, I realized that I *could* write a mystery, and I could be *good* at it, too. I enjoyed delving into the complexity of writing mysteries, the intricacy that's needed to blend intrigants, to keep readers reading and wondering and trying to figure out things until the end of the story, to make sure that at the end of the novel I not only offer a great read, but that I also create a cohesive novel. There is a concrete logic to developing the layers needed in a good mystery, and I am a very logical person. I like things in their place, and at the end of a mystery novel, all the components—someway, somehow—should connect, make sense.

All the reasons above, and so many more, are why DDIW, by far, is my most favorite writing experience. I was excited about the characters and their goings-on. There were nights when I could not stop writing because Jo and Chey, the main characters, kept me up laughing, crying, and shouting at the screen. They had a story to tell, and they were not going to let me stop until I told it. Writing DDIW sparked my desire to continue the story into a second book, and ultimately, the third in the trilogy.

> **Use the talents you have to write a story that's new to you.**

Most importantly, DDIW became my favorite writing experience because it was the first time that I broke out of my shell. And in breaking the shell, I realized that I could write in another genre and pull various parts of my talents and interests into those new stories.

It's vital that writers remember their favorite writing experiences. Just as with Day 1 and your thoughts about why you love writing, remembering your favorite writing experiences can spark the desire in you to recreate those experiences with new stories.

So, for Day 2, your goal is to reflect and journal about the following question: **what has been my favorite writing experience?**

Think of one of the stories or essays or poems you wrote that gave you your most positive writing experience. Take 10-15 minutes to think about this, and then spend 15-20 minutes journaling your response. What was the project? How did you feel while writing the project? Why is it your most favorite project? These positive feelings you write about—they will be important for you to remember when reintegrating writing into your daily life so that you can reignite your writing desires, thus bringing forth MUCH WRITING.

Find me on Facebook and/or Twitter to share your response, and use the following hashtags: #writingbloom and #favewriting.

____

____

____

____

____

____

DAY 3
FEARS THAT USURP WRITING

FEAR.

Let's just get that word out of the way now because it and all its ugly friends—worry, doubt, and anxiety to name a few—often play a role in how or why we write (or don't).

We all at some point have fears, and it seems that we creative types have them in constant, overpowering waves.

As I moved into my twenties and began to write in earnest, fear was my constant companion. Every year, there is a plethora of stories published. How was I going to compete? How was I different from or better than those who were already published? Those two questions swirled inside my head all the time. Who did I think I was to think that I was good enough for other people to want to read my work? It didn't help that

> **Fear can push us to our greatest work, or it can keep us from writing indefinitely.**

some editors recommended that I "write blacker." The fear of writing expanded to me wondering if and how I could pander to the publishing world my blackness for the sake of being published.

When you let fear in, it becomes a squatter. It comes not to visit and have some tea, a little chitchat, then leave. No, its goal is to find a nice, comfortable spot in your mind and live there forever and keep you from moving forward in your writing endeavor.

> **Fear enters and settles in with one mission: to keep you from writing.**

Even people who have the strongest confidence suffer with fear from time to time, so we can't get away from it. We can, however, fight it.

If we know what our fears are, then we can find ways to kill those fears every day. And ultimately, in the killing of those fears, some of them will die and stay dead.

> **Know your fears.**
>
> **Then obliterate them.**

When I have the fear that I'm not good enough, I go back and I read passages of *Death at the Double Inkwell* because my favorite writing experiences come from that novel. I also go back and read stories I wrote that other people enjoyed reading. I think about my MFA fiction professor, who always had such positive, motivating things to say about my work. I still have the last page of my revised thesis (a novel) where he wrote, "Shon, this is really great." That short statement meant *so* much to me, and it still warms my heart and makes me think, *Hmm, maybe I am a good writer after all*. I try to combat the fear with fact because really that's the only way you can kill a fear: obliterate it with facts.

On Day 1 of this journey, you talked about why you love writing. On Day 2, you talked about your favorite writing experience or experiences. And both are important because when you begin any journey, you want to be fueled with the awesome possibilities to come. If we started with fear, of course there's nowhere to go but up, but it puts us in a

> **Fear dies when it's shot with facts.**

downward position for the start of the journey. So, the first two days were about the things you love, the things you remember about writing that are positive.

Today's goal is **to look at fear, the fears that usurp your writing, and to think about how you can combat each fear**.

You will need about an hour to complete today's activities.

Reflect and journal on the following questions:

- → What negative thoughts do you have when you try to write?
- → Where do these negative thoughts come from? Where do they originate?

→ How true are these thoughts? Fear typically is *not* true; it's something we've conjured up in such a way that it looks real. It can even develop a physical identity because we have made it so real. Try to get outside of your negative thoughts and that place where fear exists and truly examine each of your fears, each of those negative thoughts that try to kill your writing. How real are they?

→ Write positive truths to negate each of those negative thoughts.

→ Repeat those positive truths aloud.

It will be important to keep those positive truths nearby so that you can recite them every day, several times a day if necessary, until you kill those fears.

End this journaling session with something affirming and positive so that your mind is not concluding this journaling session on negative thoughts.

Share your fears, and especially those truths, with me. Find me on Facebook and/or Twitter to share your response. Use the following hashtags: #writingbloom, #writingfears, and #writingtruths.

____

____

____

____

____

DAY 4
DAILY GOINGS-ON THAT USURP WRITING

Our negative thoughts aren't the only things that take us away from writing. Our daily goings-on can do that, too.

Every person is given 24 hours to live a day. What constitutes your 24 hours? Most of us have a million and one things to do every day, and we barely have enough time to sleep, so we are quick to say we don't have time to write. I've even said it. Shoot, I'm sure I said it today at least once.

Here's the truth though: that is *usually* a LIE. A bold-faced lie.

> **How are you using
> your 24 hours?**

So, why is this a bold-faced lie? Let's think about this for a minute. During a 24-hour day, we eat at least three times a day, we work at least 8 hours a day, we sleep hopefully about 8 hours a day, and we spend time with family and friends. But you know what else we do? We spend a great deal of time checking our phone to see if we have text messages, then to reply to those text messages. We spend a great deal of time on social media (Facebook, Twitter, Instagram, Periscope, Snapchat, and on and on). Yes, some of that time is necessary, especially if you use social media for marketing and promoting your brand, but how many times have you kept a browser tab open to Facebook while you wrote and found you spent more time posting messages, reading memes, and watching ridiculous videos than you did writing?

Don't lie.

I do it *all* the time, too, so you're not alone.

> **What are YOUR time wasters?**

We also have those moments when we sit in front of the TV and become zombified to the point where we're not even watching the TV; it's watching us. We have so many gadgets and tools that can distract us and keep us away from what we're supposed to do. In any given day, you can spend at least 1 to 3 hours checking your social media platforms and your phone, communicating things that do not benefit you at the end of the day.

So, is it possible that one of those hours could be used to write?

Make Your Writing Bloom

Most definitely.

Every one of us has at least enough time a day to write 500 words, and if you just wrote *that*, in 100 days, you would have 50,000 words, a novel.

Simply put, we have no excuse.

None.

But boy, do I have a list of them. Sometimes, as mentioned above, our daily goings-on are physical activities, such as going to work, spending time with the family. But sometimes, like for me, those goings-on are occurring in the mental. I can have a panic attack unexpectedly that will leave me exhausted and unable to function. Sometimes, my depression hits in such a way that I am unable to move—even as my mind is begging me to do so.

You may have legitimate reasons why it is hard for you to write, but if we are honest with ourselves, we'll confess that we have time killers in our lives that take priority over our writing time.

For day 4, we are going to have a venting session. You will want to set aside about an hour.

This activity asks you to **state your time killers** and **determine how you might decrease or eliminate the time used for those activities**.

You will first think about a 24-hour period in your life, and then you will **honestly journal on those**

activities that leave you with no time to write.

What time killers are in your life? How much time are these activities taking away from you?

Don't include eating, sleeping, working. We NEED those things.

What about spending time taking care of your family and their needs and projects? Typically, these are things that you NEED to do, too, but let's be real. It can't hurt to ask yourself **are there better ways I can spend time with my family and have energy and time left to write?** Because here's a truth: a good you makes for a good family. If you are not watering your spirit and passion, you die and can be of no benefit to your family.

> **A good you makes for a good family.**

Once you have journaled on these daily goings-on, reflect and journal on the following question: **how can I eliminate and/or decrease time on these activities to carve out time to write?**

To end this session on a positive note, find three writing quotes that inspire you and write them down.

Share your time killers, solutions, and quotes with me on Facebook and/or Twitter. Feel free to use the following hashtags: #writingbloom, #timekillers, and #writingquotes!

33

Make Your Writing Bloom

DAY 5
BLENDING WRITING INTO A BUSY LIFE

As an instructor, I spent a great deal of time reading and writing. I read textbooks, articles, and other content I thought would be interesting to my students. I wrote lesson plans and lectures and PowerPoints. I organized my grading schedule, and read and commented on students' work. I read and answered emails every day, even during breaks. With the heavy workload (a teacher's job doesn't end when she leaves campus), I was often left too tired to write. After grading so many papers, the thought of writing was a painful one. On top of that, I am an editor, so on any day, I can be reading, editing, and commenting on a client's work in addition to reading and grading students' work.

Words are an integral part of my life, but unfortunately, there have been days (or weeks, months, alas) when my own words do not want to come out and play.

However, I *still* must find a way to incorporate my own writing into my life.

And you do, too.

During this journey so far, we've been through the UPS of writing (days one and two) and the DOWNS that keep us from writing (days three and four).

> **Your writing deserves space within your busy life.**

Today, we take what we've learned and drop it all on the REALISTIC TABLE. You know the fears (typically not true) that keep you from writing, and you know the daily goings-on that usurp your time. Despite these negative aspects, days one and two clearly show you that you love writing and that you've had positive moments when writing.

My fears of failure (and success), the many hats I wear, and my obsessive need to check email and social media take away from my ability to write, my time to write. But when I remember the start of my love affair with writing *Death at the Double Inkwell*, the positive words of my MFA fiction professor and readers of my works, I know the truth: I'm good at what I do, and I deserve to make time for my writing.

Now that we have the truth out on the table, we have to answer this question: **how can I incorporate writing back into my life?**

Here, you will want to go back to what you wrote and thought about on days three and four about fear and daily goings-on and start thinking about how you can remove some of these things to find time to write.

Make Your Writing Bloom

Take 30 minutes to consider and journal on the following questions:

- → Is writing every day realistic to you?
- → What would be a good, consistent writing schedule for you?
- → How would you set the stage for this writing time? Will there be a particular place you write? Coffee, tea, or water? A snack to treat yourself after getting in the words?
- → How will you close out the writing time so that a) you are inspired to come back for the next writing session and b) you leave the desk feeling good about your work and yourself?

This is an important day because CONSISTENCY will be key. Once you are done this week, the goal will be to come back to Day 5, read about this consistency you envisioned, and apply it to your life for 30 days so that you are making your writing a part of your NEED-TO-DO daily goings-on.

Share some of your thoughts on blending writing into your busy life with me on Facebook and/or Twitter. Use the following hashtags: #writingbloom and #writinglife.

____

____

____

____

Make Your Writing Bloom

DAY 6
PICKING A STORY IDEA

Today, we near the end of our weeklong journey. If you have been steadfast and have stuck with me during this journey, then right now, before we even conclude, you have thought about and envisioned why you love to write; you have thought about your favorite writing experiences; you have acknowledged the fears that keep you from writing, and thought about how to combat them; you have thought about your daily living and the things that you do that might keep you from having time to write and how you might fix those issues; and you have thought about how to actually incorporate writing into your busy life.

Pat yourself on the back because you have done a lot. Now, we do something fun. We're going to take a trip through your story ideas.

Come on—we all have that folder marked STORY IDEAS, a folder full of half-finished stories, sentences, images, and words that sparked an idea but haven't been through the journey of fruition.

Make Your Writing Bloom

SO, let's take this trip, shall we?

For today's activity, you need about 90 minutes.

Take the first 15-30 minutes to go through your folder and select the top three ideas that spark you. Don't think about the spark. If you get the urge to write or at the very least think about the goings-on within that story, write it down.

Write the title of each story idea and two or three sentences that describe the story, making sure to add genre, main character, conflict, etc. So, for example, for my novella, *Saying No to the Big O*, I might write:

> *A romantic-dramedy about an oversexed woman who bets her best friend she can go a week without an orgasm. When she meets a sexy man who dismisses her advances, she pursues him and finds that there might be something better than achieving the next Big O.*

Once you've done this exercise, take 10-15 minutes to think about the pros and cons of writing each project. At the end of your time, you want to decide on the project you will write.

In the last 15-20 minutes of this activity, you will journal about your choice. Why did you select this project? What do you like about it? How excited are you to write on it?

In the last few minutes of this journaling activity, plan what you will write tomorrow on this story idea.

That's right: we're **<u>creatively writing</u>** tomorrow!

What story did you select? Tell me about it on Facebook and/or Twitter. Use the following hashtags: #writingbloom and #storyidea.

Make Your Writing Bloom

DAY 7
ROAD TRIP TO WRITING

For the last six days, you have brought thoughts and words to your temporary issue of a zestless writing regimen. You have thought about your love of writing, your best writing moments, the fears you have of writing, the things that keep you from writing, and how to incorporate writing back into your life. NOW, you are to go and work on a project.

Head to a library, a cafe, some place that has positive vibes, life, people about, and the nice dull thrum of sound that evokes productivity. Note that you will want to block out at least one hour, preferably two for this activity.

> **Write in places, spaces that spark your creativity.**

This is YOUR life and YOUR love of writing, so YOU DESERVE THIS TIME. Don't fret on it; do it.

Make Your Writing Bloom

That story idea that you wrote about yesterday? Today, you will sit and for at least one hour, you will write a minimum of 500 words toward that story.

Even if the writing is bad at the beginning, it is important to remember that writing is the key. We must start somewhere, so even if we start with not the best writing, at least you are writing, and it will start to become familiar

to you again, and you will start to embrace all the positive from past experiences of your writing, and eventually, your dry, squeaky writing will have the steady thrum of a well-oiled machine.

Once you have completed your writing, you will journal on the following questions:

- → How did you feel before you started writing?
- → How did you feel while writing?
- → How easy, difficult was it to write?
    - o Write about any difficulties and write affirmations to dismantle them.
    - o Write about what worked well for you and how you might incorporate these positive components into future writing sessions.
- → How did you feel at the completion of your writing session?
- → How have you ended this session so that you are ready to write at your next session?

How did the writing go? Let me know on Facebook and/or Twitter. Use the following hashtags: #writingbloom and #roadtripwriting.

____

____

____

____

____

____

____

____

____

____

____

____

____

____

____

Make Your Writing Bloom

Make Your Writing Bloom

WHAT NEXT?
ONE WEEK TO A LIFETIME OF WRITING

Life can change in an instant. So, if a whole life can change in the click of a BIC, surely this past week can create a change in how you think about your writing, right?

Right.

Not too long ago, I said YES. I said yes to the call on my life to use my talents as a wordsmith to sustain my livelihood. The initial steps on that road of Yes were turbulent, and even now, there are moments when fear and doubt try to steal space in my mind. However, there was a day when I sat and planned. In earnest. I had avoided planning for almost two years because I could never get my life "right" enough to finish a day's worth of to-dos, let alone a planner's worth, let alone plan anything for my writing career. But this particular day, I was determined. I marked a week of to-dos, most dealing with editing for clients.

At the end of that week, I had completed everything on my to-do lists, the first time that had happened in at least two years. The elation I felt, the energy that ran through me was incredible. And so, I did another week's worth of to-dos, this time focusing on my writing. The main goal was to finish edits to the book you are now reading. I have had the idea to write this book (and many others like it) for years, but didn't. I vowed to fulfill this dream NOW.

Every day during that week, I read, revised, rewrote, edited, tweaked this manuscript—adding more of my own life stories. Every day, fear knocked to say, "You do know that there are *so many people out there* with better credentials and more influence who talk about these same things, right?" And I would cry. And I would pause. And I would say, "You're right."

But you know what? I kept going. I fought through the fear and self-sabotage, and I finished the additions to this book.

That one week of declaring what I would do and doing it burned in me the desire to continue doing things—*my* things.

> **If writing matters to you, then you must FIGHT to keep it in your life.**

I congratulated myself after that first week. It was indeed a revelation for me, and after the second week, I reveled in the self-love from having completed this book.

And you know what I did right after? I planned another week of to-dos.

That first week invigorated me, and the second week moved me to believe I could find the love in my writing again. But that wasn't the end. Writing never ends. It takes consistent work, and with a creative endeavor such as writing, we must be very diligent and vigilant in our pursuit of time, positive thoughts, and action toward getting the work done.

The biggest piece of advice I could give you now is this: DON'T STOP WRITING.

In fact, I challenge you for the next 30 days to incorporate your schedule from Day 5 into your daily goings-on and to journal about each writing session.

In addition, I challenge you to use the small calendar on the next page to note your writing progress.

On the calendar, you will:

- → date the calendar to coincide with your next 30 days,
- → highlight the days you will be writing, and
- → put in the number of minutes for your writing session and the word count achieved.

Transfer this information into your bigger planner, your phone calendar, wherever you need it so that you see it clearly for the next 30 days.

Make Your Writing Bloom

Month:						
M	**T**	**W**	**R**	**F**	**Sa**	**Su**
—— min.	—— min.	—— min.	—— min.	—— min.	—— min.	—— min.
—— w.c.	—— w.c.	—— w.c.	—— w.c.	—— w.c.	—— w.c.	—— w.c.
—— min.	—— min.	—— min.	—— min.	—— min.	—— min.	—— min.
—— w.c.	—— w.c.	—— w.c.	—— w.c.	—— w.c.	—— w.c.	—— w.c.
—— min.	—— min.	—— min.	—— min.	—— min.	—— min.	—— min.
—— w.c.	—— w.c.	—— w.c.	—— w.c.	—— w.c.	—— w.c.	—— w.c.
—— min.	—— min.	—— min.	—— min.	—— min.	—— min.	—— min.
—— w.c.	—— w.c.	—— w.c.	—— w.c.	—— w.c.	—— w.c.	—— w.c.
—— min.	—— min.	—— min.	—— min.	—— min.	—— min.	—— min.
—— w.c.	—— w.c.	—— w.c.	—— w.c.	—— w.c.	—— w.c.	—— w.c.

Each day you write, journal on Day 7's questions:

→ How did you feel before you started writing?
→ How did you feel while writing?
→ How easy, difficult was it to write?
  o Write about any difficulties and write affirmations to dismantle them.
  o Write about what worked well for you and how you might incorporate these positive components into future writing sessions.
→ How did you feel at the completion of your writing session?
→ How have you ended this session so that you are ready to write at your next session?

Just as writing is a recursive act, this book is a recursive act as well. This journey that you have been on for the last seven days? It is not a journey that ends. It is a journey that moves forward and circles back and moves forward and circles back, on repeat. So, if you've completed this book and you feel raring to go for the next 30 days, that is awesome. If you find yourself needing a re-spark, you can return to *Make Your Writing Bloom* and rediscover what you felt when you started this book and add new notes as you go through the MYWB journey again.

I pray that this book has helped you get back to your writing. If you would like to contact me for more one-on-one assistance, email me at shon.bacon at gmail.com. Now, go forth and write on.

Make Your Writing Bloom

Make Your Writing Bloom

QUOTES THAT INSPIRE WRITING

Who doesn't love a great quote? If you're on any form of social media, every day, you see a plethora of prettily designed images full of words meant to make you think, do, and feel. I know I do.

I am a fan of quotes, especially those that inspire me to unleash my creativity, my writing.

During this journey, I asked you to find your own writing affirmations, but I also wanted to share some of my favorite quotes with you.

Below, you'll find "My Favorite Quotes" and "Bacon Bits." The former are quotes from well-known people, and the latter are my personal quotes on writing.

If you post any on social media, I would love for you to share them with me. Use the following hashtags: #writingbloom and #writingquotes!

My Favorite Quotes

Start where you are. Use what you have. Do what you can. -Arthur Ashe

---

We die. That may be the meaning of life. But we do language. That may be the measure of our lives. -Toni Morrison

---

Write the vision and make it plain on tablets, that he may run who reads it. For the vision is yet for an appointed time; but at the end it will speak, and it will not lie. Though it tarries, wait for it; because it will surely come, it will not tarry. -Habakkuk 2:2-4, NKJV

Writing is the only thing that, when I do it, I don't feel I should be doing something else. -Gloria Steinem

---

There is no greater agony than bearing an untold story inside you. -Maya Angelou

---

If there's a book that you want to read, but it hasn't been written yet, then you must write it. -Toni Morrison

---

I can shake off everything as I write; my sorrows disappear, my courage is reborn. -Anne Frank

And by the way, everything in life is writable about if you have the outgoing guts to do it, and the imagination to improvise. The worst enemy to creativity is self-doubt. -Sylvia Plath

---

A word after a word after a word is power. -Margaret Atwood

You don't start out writing good stuff. You start out writing crap and thinking it's good stuff, and then gradually you get better at it. That's why I say one of the most valuable traits is persistence. -Octavia E. Butler

Bacon Bits

You'll never have a finished book without a first sentence.

One more word on the page is one more word than you had.

If you want to write, then you must find the time to write. No one can do that for you.

Embrace mistakes. Every first draft has them.

A lot of people get so trapped by fear that they forget the first most basic and fundamental rule: put the words on the page. They will be ugly. Most writing is. But if there are no words on the page, there is nothing to edit and "make purty."

Writing is a lifelong-learning endeavor.

Every story idea is a repeat. It's your perspective that makes it unique.

Love your stories. If you don't, readers won't.

Fiction writers, think like poets. Sometimes, breaking a line can add profound meaning and mood to a story.

No writer is an island. But she can create and populate one.

NOTES

75

Make Your Writing Bloom

ABOUT THE AUTHOR

Writing evangelist Shonell Bacon endeavors to educate, entertain, and excite.

As an author, her mysteries, rom-coms, and women's fiction leave readers hungry for more. For over 17 years, she has helped 100s of writers develop their writing through her editing services and articles. As an educator, she has taught courses in English, mass communication, and fiction at the university level. As a writing coach, she has helped writers move from story idea to story completion.

When not reveling in words, Shonell is crafting, collecting pens and journals, drinking sexy java and demure teas, spending time with her family, and singing her life like a musical.

Learn more about Shonell at the following outlets:

- → Website: http://chicklitgurrl.com
- → Twitter: @chicklitgurrl
- → Facebook: http://facebook.com/shonbacon
- → Instagram: @chicklitgurrl